New Zealand
A PICTORIAL JOURNEY

text and photographs
by David Kerr

Hodder Moa Beckett

Contents

The North and South Islands of New Zealand

Cape Reinga
Parengarenga Harbour
NORTHLAND
Kaitaia
Bay of Islands
Paihia
Hokianga Harbour
Waipoua Kauri Forest
Whangarei
Dargaville

Great Barrier Island

Hauraki Gulf
Coromandel
Coromandel Peninsula
BAY OF PLENTY
EAST CAPE

AUCKLAND
Auckland

Thames
Bay of Plenty
White Island
Tauranga
Whakatane
Ruatoria

WAIKATO
Hamilton
Te Awamutu
Lake Rotorua
Mt Tarawera
Opotiki
Tokomaru Ba
Waitomo Caves
Rotorua
Tologa Bay
Te Kuiti
Lake Taupo

TARANAKI
New Plymouth
Taupo
Turangi
Lake Waikaremoana
Gisborne

Mt Taranaki
Mt Tarawera
Mt Ngauruhoe
Mt Ruapehu
Napier
Mahia Peninsula
Ohakune
Hastings
Cape Kidnappers

Wanganui
Dannevirke
HAWKE'S BAY

Farewell Spit
NELSON
Palmerston North
Kapiti Island
MANAWATU-WANGANUI

TASMAN
Tasman Bay
Masterton

Motueka
TASMAN MOUNTAINS
Nelson
Picton
Wellington
WELLINGTON
Westport
Blenheim
Cook Strait
Cape Palliser

Punakaiki
Reefton
KAIKOURA RANGES
Kaikoura
MARLBOROUGH

Greymouth
Lewis Pass
Hanmer Springs
Hokitika
Arthur's Pass

WEST COAST

Franz Josef Glacier
Fox Glacier
ALPS
Mt Cook
Christchurch
Lyttelton

Haast
SOUTHERN
Lake Tekapo
Akaroa
Lake Pukaki
Ashburton
Banks Peninsula
Mt Aspiring
Lake Wanaka
Haast Pass
Timaru
CANTERBURY
Lake Hawea

Milford Sound
Mitre Peak
Wanaka
Queenstown
Cromwell
Oamaru
Lake Wakatipu
Lake Te Anau
Alexandra
Te Anau

Otago Peninsula
Lake Manapouri
Gore
Dunedin
Balclutha
OTAGO

Invercargill
Foveaux Strait
Bluff
Catlins Coast

Stewart Island
SOUTHLAND

N

Introduction

Visitors to New Zealand will immediately be in awe of the natural beauty of its stunning landscapes. The country is a 'world in miniature', a microcosm of the world's attractions offering everything from alps and glaciers, active volcanoes and virgin rainforests, to lakes and sea coasts.

New Zealand, this isolated group of islands located in the South Pacific between the Tasman Sea and the Pacific Ocean, once formed part of Gondwanaland, the supercontinent that split apart about 80 million years ago. The split was caused by the movement of the Pacific and Indio-Australian tectonic plates. These forces created the opening of the Tasman Sea, setting New Zealand adrift, now some 2,250 kilometres east of Australia.

The largest of the islands forming New Zealand are the North Island and the South Island. In the South Island the Southern Alps rise to over three and a half kilometres above sea level. This mountain range runs the entire length of the island, interrupted briefly by three major passes through which roads have been constructed: Lewis Pass, Arthur's Pass and Haast Pass. The last of these passes is the site of a world heritage park.

A major geological feature of the North Island is its continuous thermal and volcanic activity, visible from the Volcanic Plateau in the Tongariro National Park through to White Island, the smouldering volcano that lies 51 kilometres north of Whakatane in the Pacific Ocean.

Early Polynesian voyagers arrived by canoe about 800 to 1200 years ago from the southern Cook Islands or the Society Islands — the legendary islands of Hawaiki. According to Maori legend the demi-god Maui travelled from Hawaiki and caught a huge fish on his magic hook. That huge fish was the North Island; Maui's canoe was the South Island and his anchor, Stewart Island.

In 1769 Captain James Cook circumnavigated New Zealand and mapped much of the coastline. Earlier, in 1642, Abel Tasman had already charted the west coast of both the North and South Islands. The first European settlers after Cook were sealers, who arrived in the 1790s. Permanent European settlement dates from the establishment of mission stations in the early 19th century.

New Zealand consists of many diverse regions offering dramatically different landscapes. The traveller can view mountain peaks soaring thousands of metres out of deep fiords, take a variety of trips on crystal-clear rivers, lakes and coastal waterways, or walk around active geysers bubbling away at sites of earlier volcanic destruction.

Most of New Zealand is served with a very good road network that offers access even to the very remote and secluded wilderness locations sought by the more adventurous traveller. These locations include 13 national parks and many forest parks and wildlife reserves. Some rail routes offer specially built tourist cars operating services through mountain and coastal passes. Regular ferry sailings take road and rail passengers across Cook Strait, which connects the North to the South Island.

New Zealand is not a large country, but the visitor soon discovers there is a great deal to see and do. As well as exploring the forests, mountains, lakes and beaches, there's a huge range of activities available, from whale watching to white-water rafting, from the sedate to the adventurous.

New Zealand's cities have a growing cultural life, and arts, crafts and heritage trails are popular. You'll also find plenty of fresh air, fresh food and fine wines — and friendly local people.

Northland and the Bay of Islands

Locals often refer to Northland as 'the Winterless North' because it enjoys warmer than average temperatures for New Zealand. From Auckland, the main tourist route to Northland and the Far North is the Twin Coast Highway which leads up the rugged west coast and the Kauri Coast. Here you can drive through the Waipoua Forest and see giant kauri trees more than a thousand years old.

Opposite: The golden beaches and sweeping bays of Moturua Island provide the ideal setting for summer boating activity.

Below: A tourist catamaran emerges out of the Hole in the Rock near Cape Brett in the Bay of Islands.

The road runs north to the Hokianga Harbour, with its spectacular sand dunes on the northern side of the heads. Inland at Rawene a ferry crosses the harbour, linking to the road to Kaitaia. From here the road continues to New Zealand's northernmost point, Cape Reinga, with its lighthouse overlooking the converging waters of the Tasman Sea and the Pacific Ocean. To the south-west along the coast is Cape Maria Van Diemen and to the east, North Cape.

Along the east coast from Kaitaia are vistas of spectacular golden beaches with fine blond silica sand, unique to the beaches of the Far North. A common sight in the Far North are nikau palms and pohutukawa trees. The pohutukawa is known as New Zealand's Christmas tree because it is covered in crimson blossoms in December.

Further south lies Kerikeri, the town central to the region often described as 'the Fruit Bowl of the North'. Just south of Kerikeri lie Waitangi and Paihia, the gateway to the wide-open waterways of the Bay of Islands Maritime Park. This outdoor adventure playground is a popular destination,

Right: The lighthouse at New Zealand's northernmost point, Cape Reinga.

Below: Omapere Wharf at Martins Bay on the Hokianga Harbour with the dramatic sand dunes on the northern side of the harbour.

Opposite: A majestic crimson pohutukawa tree above the wide-open waterways of the Bay of Islands.

with its semi-tropical temperatures, the aqua blue of the Pacific Ocean, and many golden beaches in sheltered inlets and islands. Holiday-makers are attracted by dolphin- and whale-watching, deep-sea fishing and the many other activities summer brings. Trophy marlin fishing attracts enthusiasts from the world over to these famed game-fishing waters.

Waitangi, now a historical reserve, was where the Treaty of Waitangi was signed on 6 February 1840, making New Zealand part of the British Empire. Across the water from Paihia is the historic seaside village of Russell, originally known as Kororareka. Established around 1800, Russell was New Zealand's first European settlement, its first capital and its oldest town. It is renowned as a big-game fishing centre and as a holiday destination of major historical interest. With many of the original buildings on the seafront still standing, the restaurants and shops of Russell create an atmosphere reminiscent of its history.

Just south of Paihia is a small town called Kawakawa where you will find the famous public toilets designed and constructed by internationally acclaimed Austrian artist, the late Friedensreich Hundertwasser.

Along the Northland coastline just south of the city of Whangarei are spectacular views of the Hen and Chickens, Little Barrier and Great Barrier Islands. These islands form the outer barriers of the Hauraki Gulf, which extends as far south as the Firth of Thames, at the southern end of the Coromandel Peninsula.

Right: Whare Runanga meeting house on the grounds of Waitangi near Paihia.

Below: Late afternoon sun casts a warm glow over the historic buildings on The Strand on the Russell waterfront.

Opposite: 'Tane Mahuta', New Zealand's tallest kauri tree, thought to be around 1200 years old, located in the Waipoua State Forest, south of the Hokianga Harbour on Northland's west coast.

The alluring blue waters of the Pacific Ocean wash the blond silica sands at the mouth of Parengarenga Harbour, at the northern end of Great Exhibition Bay.

Auckland

Greater Auckland is New Zealand's largest city. It spreads from the Bombay Hills and Franklin County in the south as far north as Warkworth, taking in the Whangaparaoa Peninsula and islands in the Hauraki Gulf. It boasts over 50 islands, 22 regional parks and three marine reserves, as well as many bays and beaches. Nestled between the Waitemata Harbour to the north and the Manukau Harbour to the west, Auckland is known as 'the City of Sails' for the myriad craft of all descriptions seen on the water all year round.

Opposite: Westhaven Marina and its hundreds of watercraft, with downtown Auckland in the background.

Below: Auckland Harbour Bridge and the highrise panorama of Auckland city.

More than 50 volcanic cones are scattered around the Auckland area. The largest, Rangitoto Island, can be reached by ferry from downtown Auckland. There you can explore the regenerating pohutukawa forest, the lava caves and enjoy the spectacular view from the summit.

The Auckland skyline is dominated by the Sky Tower, which at 328 metres is the tallest building in the southern hemisphere. Superb views are to be had from the tower and also from the summits of Mt Eden and One Tree Hill.

Some points of interest in the central city are Queen Street, the Auckland War Memorial Museum in the picturesque Domain, Auckland Town Hall and the Aotea Centre, the magical Civic Theatre, built in 1929 and recently restored, the Auckland City Art Gallery and the Old Custom House. Through Albert Park lies the University of Auckland with its distinctive clock tower.

The Viaduct Basin, where the America's Cup yacht syndicates were based during the America's Cup challenges and defences, is situated on the waterfront. The New Zealand National Maritime Museum is

also here, where an amazing collection of memorabilia of New Zealand's boating heritage is displayed. Harbour cruises leave regularly from the Old Ferry Building, as do ferries to Devonport on the North Shore or to islands in the Hauraki Gulf.

One of the most scenic urban drives from downtown Auckland is along Tamaki Drive to the eastern suburbs of Orakei, Mission Bay, Kohimarama and St Heliers.

To the north of Auckland over the harbour bridge lies Wenderholm Regional Park, Waiwera Thermal Hot Pools and the Whangaparaoa Peninsula, where there is a world-renowned golf course at the Gulf Harbour Country Club. Further north is the small town of Warkworth, and on the coast at Leigh is the Goat Island Marine Reserve.

West of Auckland is a thriving vineyard area, and the rugged, wild beaches of the west coast, such as Piha or Muriwai, with their characteristic black sand and huge waves.

Heading south of the city, Otara Market every Saturday morning provides an opportunity to see the diversity of Auckland's multicultural community.

Above: Dinghies 'up on the hard' at the Royal Akarana Yacht Club, Okahu Bay.

Opposite above: The lone Obelisk dominates the volcano of One Tree Hill.

Opposite below: Auckland War Memorial Museum in the Auckland Domain, which overlooks Auckland Harbour.

Right: The quaint shops of Parnell Village near the Auckland War Memorial Museum.

Below: The Old Ferry Building at the bottom of Queen Street on the Auckland waterfront.

Opposite above: The aqua blue waters of the Pacific Ocean lap the golden sands at Palm Beach on Waiheke Island.

Opposite below: The rugged west coast beach of Piha.

The Coromandel Peninsula

The Coromandel Peninsula juts out from south of Auckland and separates the Hauraki Gulf from the Bay of Plenty. The peninsula forms part of the greater Hauraki Gulf Maritime Park, which includes the eastern seaboard down as far as Waihi Beach. The Coromandel and Moehau ranges form the backbone of the peninsula, running its entire length and ending at Port Jackson.

These ranges often act as a barrier protecting the east coast from inclement weather from the Hauraki Gulf and the south-west. The landscape of the peninsula is full of dramatic contrasts, ranging from rugged mountains to undulating hills and rocky coastline.

The Coromandel Peninsula was the scene of New Zealand's first goldrush after gold was discovered near Waihi in 1852. Gold stamping batteries can be found near the township of Thames, the gateway to the Peninsula, and further north at Coromandel township.

Opposite: Beachgoers enjoy the warm summer temperatures walking through 'the cathedral' at Cathedral Cove.

Below: Holidaymakers enjoying the low tide at Whitianga Harbour.

The early 1880s saw the uncontrolled exploitation of the area's kauri trees and kauri gum. Abandoned mining and timber-milling machinery can still be found deep in the bush. The kauri forests were felled by overseas timber traders, leaving little of the original native forest standing. Some of the timber was used to build dams to float logs down to the coastal lowlands for shipping. A few kauri driving dams still remain, one near Thames and one on Great Barrier Island, which lies

Right: Lush tropical nikau palms rise above the sweeping curve of Waikawau Bay on the east coast of the peninsula.

Opposite: Coromandel's intricate island-studded coastline near the entrance to Manaia Harbour on the western seaboard.

off the tip of the peninsula. Despite the heavy timber-felling, some spectacular old kauri trees can still be seen on the peninsula and, with recent conservation efforts, reforestation is occurring.

The west and east coasts of the Coromandel are linked by four main routes. Although these roads are winding, narrow and often unsealed, they provide an interesting drive through the ranges. The main highway forms part of the greater Pacific Coast Highway, which runs from Auckland to the Coromandel Peninsula and the Bay of Plenty and around the East Cape to Hawke's Bay.

The indented coastline is studded with many offshore islands, making for a spectacular seascape, especially near the mouth of Coromandel Harbour. The coastline offers a variety of inviting beaches, such as Cathedral Cove near Whitianga and Hahei Beach on the east coast of the peninsula.

During the months of November, December and January pohutukawa can be seen blooming in abundance up and down the coastline.

With its mild, warm climate the region is an ideal holiday destination, offering a great variety of outdoor activities including coastal kayaking around the whole peninsula, boogie boarding and surfing at some of the great surf beaches, and fishing from beach, rocks or boat. For the more energetic, there are a number of excellent tramping destinations such as Castle Rock, which gives spectacular views westward over Coromandel township and the Hauraki Gulf and eastward to Matarangi and the east coast. As well as motels and private rental houses, there are a number of camping grounds on the peninsula, ranging from the very well-equipped to basic back-to-nature facilities run by the Department of Conservation.

The largest town on the peninsula is Thames, an old goldmining town. From here the scenic coastal road winds up to Coromandel township, where Driving Creek Railway, high on the hills just out of town, provides an hour-long round trip. The railway, which crosses trestle bridges, climbs spirals and travels through tunnels, was originally built by Ceramic artist Barry Brickell as a means of transporting clay downhill to his kiln.

The road continues north of Coromandel through Colville and up to Port Charles and Port Jackson, then round by Waikawau Bay and Kennedy Bay, looping back to Coromandel town. From here, the highway cuts across the ranges to Whitianga, via Whangapoua Harbour and Matarangi Beach, offering magnificent views of Coromandel Harbour and Mercury Bay. At Whitianga a ferry takes visitors across to Ferry Landing near Cook's Beach, a popular destination for holidaymakers. Further south are Hahei Beach and Hot Water Beach — the latter so called because of the hot springs that seep up through the sand at the cliff face. Between mid and low tides visitors can scoop or dig their own hot pools in the sand and then cool off in the sea. From Whitianga the road continues south to the coastal resort towns of Tairua, Pauanui, Whangamata, Waihi and Waihi Beach.

Right: A fishing fleet tied up at Coromandel Harbour.

Below: Late afternoon sun casts shadows across Whanganui Island at the entrance to Coromandel Harbour.

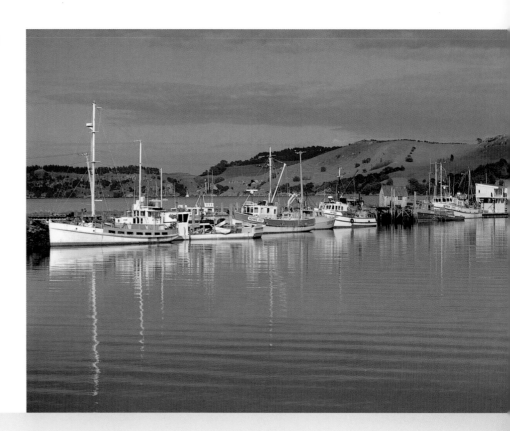

Right: Driving Creek Railway winding its way uphill above the township of Coromandel.

Below: The historic Brian Boru Hotel at Thames.

Bottom: Ocean Beach, Tairua.

Waikato and the King Country

The Waikato district is well known for its rich dairy farmlands and horse studs. The district takes its name from the mighty Waikato River, which, at 354 kilometres in length, is New Zealand's longest.

The Waikato flows north from Lake Taupo in the Volcanic Plateau via Hamilton to the river mouth at Port Waikato, on the west coast just south of Auckland's Manukau Harbour. South of Hamilton, dams for hydroelectric power stations have formed three picturesque lakes.

Just north of Hamilton is Ngaruawahia, the headquarters of the 19th-century Maori King Movement. Here the Maori Queen, Te Arikinui Dame Te Atairangikaahu, has her official house, the Turongo residence, at the Turangawaewae marae. Just north of Ngaruawahia and near Huntly is Taupiri Mountain, a historic burial site for both Maori royalty and the tribal people.

To the south of Hamilton lies the picturesque township of Cambridge with its beautiful trees and antique and craft shops. Around the Cambridge area you will see many horse breeding studs. This area is renowned for having produced many international thoroughbreds.

The city of Hamilton, on the Waikato River, is the region's major centre and the country's largest inland city. Cruises on the *Waipa Delta* paddleboat give visitors a picturesque view of the city and the surrounding rural district.

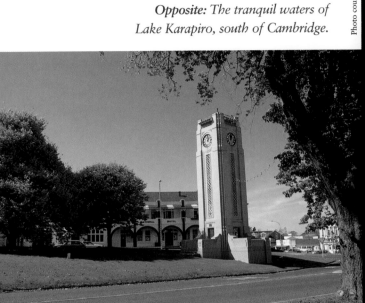

Photo courtesy of Tourism Holdings Ltd

Right: Visitors enjoy a boat cruise through the Waitomo Caves with glow-worms providing a spectacular display.

Below: A Cambridge street ablaze with autumn colour.

Opposite: The tranquil waters of Lake Karapiro, south of Cambridge.

About three quarters of an hour south of Hamilton lies the country town of Tirau. Here two buildings are constructed out of corrugated iron (a commonly used farm building material) in the shapes of a giant sheepdog and sheep. These reflect the rural nature of Tirau and its strong farming community. The dog is the local information centre and the sheep is a wool gallery selling sheep and wool products.

Beneath the rugged King Country farmlands, seventy-five kilometres south of Hamilton on State Highway 3 towards New Plymouth, are the world-famous Waitomo Caves. These weatherworn limestone formations provide a magic display of glow-worms on the ceilings and upper walls of the caves. At the local Waitomo Museum of Caves you will find interesting displays explaining the history of the caving system and showing memorabilia of the region.

Other major attractions at Waitomo include the more exciting activities such as blackwater rafting in tyre tubes down the caves' tunnels and streams, and abseiling down the mighty shaft at Lost World.

Not far from Waitomo, on the coast road to Marokopa, you will find the majestic Marokopa Falls and the Natural Bridge, a remarkable 15-metre limestone arch that bridges the Mangapohue Stream. This bridge is all that remains of an underground river channel; the rest of the cave collapsed and eroded away thousands of years ago.

Twenty minutes south of the Waitomo Caves lies Te Kuiti, a typical rural town in the heart of the King Country which has become known as The Sheep Shearing Capital of the World. At the southern end of the town you can view a giant statue of a sheep shearer in action. Further south on State Highway 3 you will drive through the rugged King Country terrain to eventually meet the coastline of the North Taranaki Bight. Here on a fine day it is possible to see the spectacular sight of Mt Egmont (2,518 metres), also known as Mt Taranaki, rising above the distant coastal horizon.

Rotorua

Rotorua, home of the Te Arawa tribe, is located on the North Island's thermal belt, which stretches from White Island, in the Pacific Ocean off the coast of Whakatane, south to the mountains in the Tongariro National Park, on the North Island's Volcanic Plateau.

Opposite: The silica terrace of the Champagne Pool at Waiotapu Thermal Wonderland.

Below: St Faith's Anglican Church beyond the decorated entrance way.

Below right: Rotorua has a large Maori population, whose cultural activities are a major attraction.

The area around Rotorua is internationally renowned for its thermal activity. Here you will find magnificent examples of bubbling mud, hot mineral pools, spouting geysers, and fumaroles (vents) steaming in a magical landscape first wrought by violent volcanic activity many thousands of years ago.

On the northern approach to Rotorua are two popular attractions, the Agrodome, with its live display of sheep farming, and Rainbow Springs, where many of New Zealand's unique native plants and animals can be observed.

Situated on the edge of the lake itself is Ohinemutu, the original Maori settlement, around which the town of Rotorua grew. The village's St Faith's Anglican Church, built in 1910, is embellished with Maori carvings and tukutuku lattice panels and features a sand-blasted window depicting Christ dressed in a korowai (the cloak of a chief) walking on the water of Lake Rotorua.

Lake Rotorua and the island of Mokoia are associated with a great Maori legend, the love story of Hinemoa and Tutanekai. Hinemoa lived on the shores of Lake Rotorua. She fell in love with Tutanekai, who lived on Mokoia Island, but the match did not meet with her

family's approval. The lovers arranged for Hinemoa to sail to Mokoia Island by canoe at night while Tutanekai played his flute to guide her. Her family discovered this plan and hid the canoe. In desperation Hinemoa attached gourds to herself and swam to the island where she was united with Tutanekai.

In the town centre, within the elegant Government Gardens is the historic Tudor-style Bath House, an architectural reminder of Rotorua's colonial past, which houses the Rotorua Museum of Art and History, Te Whare Taonga o Te Arawa. On the outskirts of Rotorua lies the thermal village of Whakarewarewa which offers the opportunity to sample the splendours of bubbling mud pools and gushing geysers, and experience a little of Maori culture. Here Maori carvers and weavers demonstrate their skills and visitors are welcome to enjoy a colourful concert party, or a hangi, a Maori feast cooked in the ground using hot stones.

Another spectacular thermal area is Waiotapu Thermal Wonderland, about two minutes' drive south of Waimangu Valley. A walk through native forest leads to volcanic craters, bubbling mud pools, silica terraces and the towering Lady Knox Geyser, then on to the Artist's Palette, a thermal lake of many different colours, and the beautiful Champagne Pool.

Lake Rotorua is one of 14 picturesque lakes in the area, all of which offer excellent trout fishing and boating. Lake Tarawera is the most spectacular, with the volcanic dome of Mt Tarawera forming a dramatic backdrop. This was the site of the famous eruption on 10 June 1886 which buried a Maori village under nearly two and a half metres of volcanic mud and ash and destroyed the famous Pink and White Terraces, two beautiful enormous silica formations on the shores of Lake Rotomahana. The terraces were considered one of the wonders of the world, and gained enormous popularity among tourists from all over the world in the 19th century. The Buried Village at Te Wairoa, once the starting point for visits to the Pink and White Terraces, features a small museum with photographs taken both before and after the disaster, the ruins of a hotel and flour mill, and a stone pataka (storehouse). The scenic road to the Buried Village from Rotorua passes the Whakarewarewa Forest, with its redwood grove, and the picturesque Blue and Green Lakes.

Opposite left: Visitors enter
Whakarewarewa Thermal
Reserve to veiw the amazing
thermal activity.

Opposite right: Pohutu
Geyser spurts hot water over
20 metres into the air
at Whakarewarewa
Thermal Reserve.

Left: The tranquil Blue Lake.

Below: The entrance to
Tamaki Maori Village where
visitors can experience
Maori culture and hospitality
in a Maori village.

Above: The Tudor-style Bath House overlooking Government Gardens.

Right: Sunrise over Lake Tarawera. The region is world renowned for its trout fishing.

Below: The Rotorua gondola rises 900 metres up the slopes of Mt Ngongotaha to give breathtaking views over Rotorua city and Lake Rotorua.

The Volcanic Plateau and Taranaki

The Volcanic Plateau lies at the centre of the North Island and is an area rich in unspoilt natural beauty. It is dominated by the spectacular mountain peaks of Ruapehu, Ngauruhoe and Tongariro, and the grandeur of Lake Taupo, New Zealand's largest lake. The lake has formed in the crater left by enormous eruptions, most recently 1800 years ago. The lake flows out near Taupo township to form the mighty Waikato River, New Zealand's longest river.

Opposite: The cone of Mt Ngauruhoe dominates State Highway 47 in the Tongariro National Park.

Below: Thrill-seekers enjoy an exciting manoeuvre at the Huka Falls near Taupo.

The northern approach to Taupo is breathtaking. It runs past the steaming landscape of Wairakei to the Huka Falls with its thundering cascade of water. The town of Taupo nestles by the lake at the foothills of Mt Tauhara with the majestic peaks of Ruapehu, Ngauruhoe and Tongariro in the distance.

Taupo is probably best known for its trout fishing. It is over one hundred years since the first trout fry were released into the region and today it draws anglers from all over the world. On the western side of Lake Taupo is Pureora Forest Park, with rare birds such as the kaka and kokako. To the south-east of the lake is the Kaimanawa Forest Park, which contains large, ancient beech forests and is well known for its tramping tracks.

To the south of the lake is the Tongariro National Park, New Zealand's first national park and a world heritage area. Tongariro Crossing is considered to be the best one-day walk in New Zealand. The 17-kilometre walk takes you past mountain springs, emerald

lakes, active volcanoes and lava flows, and offers superb 180-degree views. In 1887 the three volcanoes of Ruapehu (2,797 metres), Tongariro (1,968 metres) and Ngauruhoe (2,291 metres) were gifted to the people of New Zealand by Ngati Tuwharetoa, the local Maori tribe, to create this park. The volcanoes of the Tongariro National Park lie at the end of a volcanic chain that extends north from here through White Island and the Kermadec Islands to the islands of Tonga in the Pacific. These peaks are particularly striking as they rise from a stark plateau of tussock and desert, and from the south-west in winter when snow and ice contrast beautifully with the dense forest.

The largest of the three volcanoes, Ruapehu, has three ski-fields on its slopes. At the base of Whakapapa, the largest of the ski-fields, lies the majestic Grand Chateau, built in 1929. On the southern slopes is Turoa ski-field, just above Ohakune. The third ski-field is Tukino, on the eastern side of the mountain.

The township of Turangi, about 45 minutes from Whakapapa, grew from a tiny fishing retreat. Above the town is the graceful Mt Pihanga. According to Maori mythology, Pihanga is a female mountain whose charm led the male mountains around her to fight over her. When Tongariro won her love the other mountains had to go — Mt Taranaki to Taranaki, Mt Putauaki to the Bay of Plenty and Mt Tauhara to the north-east of Lake Taupo. Intriguing places to visit from Turangi are the Tongariro fish hatchery, the Army Museum at Waiouru and the hot pools at Tokaanu, to the west of Turangi.

A catamaran plies the deep blue waters of Lake Taupo with the dramatic backdrop of Mts Tongariro, Ngauruhoe and Ruapehu in the background.

Right: Sunset behind the majestic peak of Mt Egmont/Taranaki.

Below: Crystal clear streams flowing below Mt Ngauruhoe.

Bottom: Snow on the tussock plains of the Tongariro National Park.

Mt Ruapehu is the highest and most active of the North Island volcanoes, with the most spectacular recent eruptions occuring in 1996.

Bay of Plenty
and the East Cape

The Bay of Plenty, known as 'the Fruit Bowl of New Zealand' is renowned for its rich soil and temperate climate, which help to produce much of the country's citrus fruit, kiwifruit, tamarillos, feijoas and avocados.

Below: The seaside resort of Mt Maunganui, with Matakana Island lying directly behind the volcanic cone of Mt Maunganui.

Opposite: The constantly fuming volcanic White Island lies 51 kilometres off the coast from Whakatane in the western Bay of Plenty.

Tauranga is the largest city in the Bay of Plenty and its port at Mt Maunganui is one of New Zealand's largest export ports. The whole coastal region is steeped in Maori history, with many pa sites (fortified Maori villages), such as the one at Mt Maunganui or at Gate Pa. Te Puke, about 30 kilometres south-east of Tauranga, is a flourishing fruit-growing and dairying centre, and is known as 'the kiwifruit capital of the world'.

The route from the Bay of Plenty to the East Cape follows the Pacific Coast Highway to Opotiki and Gisborne and is at its scenic best around Christmas when the pohutukawa are in full bloom. About 70 kilometres from Opotiki is Te Kaha, set in a beautiful cove, one of the most picturesque on the cape. This area was the scene of many fierce intertribal battles between the Ngati Apanui and Ngati Porou tribes. In the 1830s many whalers moved to the East Cape from the Bay of Islands and intensive whaling was carried out with the whales being landed on the beach.

From Te Kaha the road continues to Whanarua Bay and Waihau Bay with its guest house and licensed restaurant, established in 1914, which looks across the bay to Cape Runaway. Twelve kilometres further east is Whangaparaoa (the bay of whales), where the Maori canoes *Arawa* and *Tainui* first landed in New Zealand from Hawaiki. There was disgreement about who had landed first and could lay claim to whales stranded on the beach. The Tainui won and the Arawa moved on to the Bay of Plenty. The Tainui are said to have introduced the kumara (sweet potato) to New Zealand.

Hicks Bay, named by Captain Cook in 1769 after one of his officers, has become popular with campers as a stopover on the journey around the cape. The derelict remains of the freezing works near the wharf are a reminder of the days of busy coastal shipping on the cape before roads were properly developed. During the 1920s there were freezing works at Hicks Bay, Tokomaru Bay and Gisborne. Wharves were built at all three locations and also at Tolaga Bay. The Tolaga Bay pier remains New Zealand's longest at 660 metres (2,165 feet). The closure of the freezing works in the region has adversely affected the local economy, however forestry now plays a large part in the region's survival.

Twenty-one kilometres east of Te Araroa is the East Cape Lighthouse, which marks the most easterly point of the mainland of New Zealand. Inland from Ruatoria lies Mt Hikurangi (1,839 metres), which is the first landmark in the country to see the light each day.

Tokomaru Bay, like Tolaga Bay and Waipiro Bay, was once a centre of commercial activity. Between Tokomaru Bay and Tolaga Bay lies Anaura Bay. It has a wonderful golden sandy beach where Captain Cook landed for the second time in New Zealand. The Anaura Bay walkway is about three and a half kilometres long and offers a panoramic view of the area.

Proudly standing on Kaiti Hill above Gisborne is a memorial statue of Captain Cook. Behind him across Poverty Bay is a headland, Young Nicks Head, named after the cabin boy on the *Endeavour* who was the first aboard to sight New Zealand in 1769.

Gisborne is situated on Poverty Bay at the mouth of the Turanganui River. Despite its name, the Poverty Bay region is one of rich land that makes it ideal for growing crops and fruit. The hill country is well suited to farming sheep, cattle and deer. With its shingly soil and temperate climate, the Gisborne region also produces much of New Zealand's wine.

Right: *The vivid colours of the Pacific at Tokomaru Bay.*

Below: *New Zealand's longest pier stretches 660 metres out into the calm waters of Tolaga Bay.*

Opposite above: *Lake Waikaremoana in Te Urewera National Park.*

Opposite below: *The statue of Captain Cook with the headland of Young Nicks Head in the background across Poverty Bay.*

Hawke's Bay

Napier and Hastings (twin cities less than twenty minutes apart) are approximately five hours' drive from Auckland, four from Wellington. The Hawke's Bay climate has a Mediterranean feel to it as temperatures are normally two to three degrees warmer here than in other parts of the North Island. This warmer climate is ideal for pipfruit and grape growing, and the region prides itself on the many international award-winning premium wines it produces.

Napier and Hastings are accessible via the Pacific Coast Highway from Gisborne, the Mahia Peninsula and Wairoa, through native forests and the Lake Tutira Bird Sanctuary. When you pass through Wairoa, take the road out to Lake Waikaremoana in Te Urerewa National Park. This tranquil area is popular for its trout fishing, boating, kayaking, day walks or longer tramps around the lake and the surrounding Urewera mountains.

Approaching Hawke's Bay from the north on the Thermal Explorer Highway from Taupo, you are treated to splendid views of the Pacific Ocean as you descend from the ridge of the Maungaharuru Range into the Esk Valley. Napier is the first city you reach after passing through the Esk Valley wine-growing area from the north.

To reach Hawke's Bay from the south, the choice is between State Highway 50, which is very scenic, or the quicker route on State Highway 2 via Waipukurau and Waipawa.

Now spread around and onto Bluff Hill, a major landmark on the horizon, Napier used to be almost completely surrounded by water. This was before the great earthquakes of 1931 all but flattened both Napier and nearby Hastings while raising over 2,000 hectares of seabed from the ocean to become dry land. Both cities were reduced to rubble and 258 people died in this, New Zealand's greatest, catastrophe.

The city of Napier had to be almost completely rebuilt, and was reconstructed in the then current 'Art Deco' style of architecture for which it is now renowned. Daily guided walking tours highlight buildings of interest and during February of each year there is an Art Deco weekend, which features a vintage car parade, jazz bands, a biplane swoop, and other exhibitions and entertainment with a 1930s theme. The Hawke's Bay Museum, between Herschell Street and Marine Parade, has a fascinating display of local history that includes an audiovisual of the devastating earthquake of 1931. The Art Deco Trust has a retail shop that offers a full range of Art Deco souvenirs and memorabilia. A fine example of Napier's Art Deco architecture is the Rothman's of Pall Mall building situated some distance from the

Left: Intricate Art Deco architecture details the fine old 'Rothmans of Pall Mall' building in Napier city.

Opposite: The Coleraine Vineyard of the Te Mata Estate is one of many vineyards in the Hawke's Bay region renowned for its premium quality wines.

city centre, on the corner of Bridge and Ossian Streets in Ahuriri near the Napier marina.

Bluff Hill Lookout offers spectacular views of the Hawke's Bay coastline north to Mahia Peninsula and south to Cape Kidnappers.

There are three statues on Napier's tree-lined Parade: the 'Spirit of Napier', in the south; fishermen hauling their catch, by the Aquarium; and 'Pania of the Reef'. The Maori legend has it that Pania was a member of the Sea People and left them to live on land with her human lover, Karitoki. Her family constantly called to her to come home and finally she could not resist them and swam to meet them one last time. They would not let her return to land and pulled her into the depths of the sea. Today when you pass over the reef, you can imagine you can see her with arms outstretched trying to return to her lover.

Hastings, a city of parks and gardens situated on the Heretaunga Plains, is Napier's twin city. Napier's port handles all the goods leaving the Hastings area. The earthquake of 1931 affected Hastings too and this city also has many highly decorative buildings constructed in the Spanish Mission and Art Deco styles. Take a pleasant walk through the Frimley Rose Garden, where there are more than five thousand rose bushes and rare species of trees, or in Cornwall Park, which features the Osmanthus Chinese Garden. For those looking for excitement, try New Zealand's first full-themed water park, Splash Planet, where there is plenty of year-round fun. For others there is Fantasyland, an unusual children's playground with fairy-tale castle, pirate ship, moon rocket and many other fantastic structures.

While in this area it is a good idea to take one of the many tours to Cape Kidnappers to see the world's largest mainland gannet colony. These tours include transport by four-wheel-drive vehicles, tractors and Unimogs along the beach or over farmland. The colony of nesting Australasian gannets is administered by the Department of Conservation and presents an opportunity to see these birds in their own environment.

Past Hastings to the south-east you will travel through the picturesque village of Havelock North. From there, visit Te Mata Peak, which offers some of the finest views in Hawke's Bay — inland to the Ruahine, Kaweka and Maungaharuru ranges, with Ruapehu in the central North Island in the distance, and facing the sea to Mahia Peninsula, Tukituki River and Cape Kidnappers.

While in Hawke's Bay take one of the many wine tours or visit the vineyards independently. There are a great number to visit, many with dining facilities. Visit Porangahau out on the coast from Waipukurau, famous for its diving, snorkelling, fishing, waterskiing and surfing. Explore Te Angiangi Marine Reserve.

Heading north from Napier towards Taupo, you will drive through a variety of landscapes ranging from the beautiful Esk Valley with its many lush vineyards to the desert-like lands near Rangitaiki, from gentle plains to two rugged mountain ranges (Maungaharuru and Ahimanawa), and through forests and farmland.

Right: 'Pania of the Reef', one of three statues on Napier's tree-lined Parade.

Below: Early morning sun lights the barren ridge of Te Mata Peak, with the Tukituki River winding its way behind.

Opposite: The splendid ocean vista of the Napier seafront with Cape Kidnappers on the horizon.

The parched amber hills of Havelock North

Wellington and the Wairarapa

Wellington is New Zealand's capital city. It stands on the North Island's south-west tip, with Cook Strait separating it from the South Island. Because of its position, exposed to Cook Strait and the southerly winds off the South Island, the city is often referred to as 'Windy Wellington'. The inter-island and fast ferries ply the Cook Strait in all weathers to carry motorists and passengers between Wellington and Picton, at the top of the South Island.

Opposite: The Kelburn Cable Car, which was originally built in 1902, climbs steeply up the hills high above Wellington.

Below: Parliament House and the 'Beehive', New Zealand's 'hive' of politics.

Maori legend has it that Maui, out fishing with his brothers, hauled up a great fish, the North Island. The mouth of this great fish was Te Whanganui-a-Tara (the Great Harbour of Tara) which was later inhabited by the Ngati Tara for over a thousand years. The British called this harbour Port Nicholson initially, then changed its name to Wellington as a tribute to the Duke of Wellington. Like many New Zealand towns it began as a whaling centre, but gradually other industries grew. The seat of government was moved from Auckland (then and now New Zealand's largest city) to Wellington in 1865 because of its central position in New Zealand.

Nowadays, Wellington is a bustling, cosmopolitan city with a character all its own, enclosed by the unbroken hills surrounding Port Nicholson. The city's surviving early 19th-century architecture contrasts with the modern high-rise towers of the business world now overlooking Wellington's deep-water harbour.

Pleasure craft moored at Oriental Bay below the house-studded hill of Mt Victoria.

Fur seals basking on the rocks at Cape Palliser in the southern Wairarapa.

The Rimutaka Range separates Wellington from the rural landscape and country lifestyle of the Wairarapa, which has become an increasingly popular weekend retreat for many Wellingtonians and others to enjoy. The Wairarapa has grown an international reputation for its many vineyards and exclusive country estate boutique lodges. The coastline is rugged and wild in places, with spectacular views across the pounding surf to the South Island.

At the southernmost point of the North Island is Cape Palliser where you will find a very large seal colony, with seals sometimes lying beside the road. Further on, high on the headland, is a lighthouse that can be reached by walking up the hundreds of steps to the top. Just before you reach the cape you will pass through the tiny fishing village of Te Humenga, where you will see an interesting collection of large robust tractors and trailers that carry large fishing vessels to ply the savage coastal waters of the area. Other attractions nearby are the Putangirua Pinnacles, a unique rock formation, picturesque Lake Wairarapa, and, further up the Wairarapa coast past the town of Masterton, Castle Point Lighthouse. The only towns in the Wairarapa region are Martinborough, Featherston, Greytown and Masterton.

The only flat land in Wellington itself is the waterfront and the main shopping area around Lambton Quay, Willis Street and Courtenay Place.

The Wellington waterfront has developed over time with many of the wharves and shipping areas now devoted to 'cosmopolitan lifestyle' cafés, bars and restaurants. The entire waterfront area has been developed to connect the downtown Wellington business district to Oriental Parade and the national museum, Te Papa. This museum has one of the best collections of art and artefacts in the South Pacific.

Marlborough, Kaikoura and Nelson

The Marlborough–Kaikoura region stretches from the idyllic, brilliant blue- and green-coloured waterways of the Marlborough Sounds down the east coast to the Kaikoura Peninsula in the south.

The Marlborough Sounds are made up of many intricate waterways, the largest of which is Queen Charlotte Sound, which is the sea passage for all shipping connecting Wellington to Picton at the head of the sound. The drive from Picton to Havelock via Queen Charlotte Drive has breathtaking views of bays and beaches along Queen Charlotte and Mahau sounds.

Twenty-nine kilometres south of Picton lies the town of Blenheim, at the base of the Wairau Plains. Against a dramatic backdrop of burnt amber ranges high above the plains, this wide expanse with its warm, dry climate is ideal for grape growing. There are many award-winning wine-producing vineyards here. The biggest of these is the Montana Brancott Estate.

South of Blenheim lies the seaside town of Kaikoura. The seafloor drops steeply away from the land here forming part of a huge deep-water canyon that runs from Antarctica past Kaikoura and into the Pacific Ocean. Sperm, humpback and southern right whales (and occasionally orca, killer whales) can be viewed close to the coastline as they migrate up and down these waters.

Left: Marlborough is New Zealand's largest wine-producing region, home to wineries and vineyards like the Brancott Estate.

Opposite: *Sunset casts silhouetted shapes with fingers of land reaching out into Queen Charlotte Sound.*

The Nelson region encompasses the north-western half of the top of the South Island. It has three national parks (Abel Tasman, Kahurangi and Nelson Lakes) and two marine reserves. One of the best-known walks is the Heaphy Track, which takes four to five days and leads through the Kahurangi National Park with its glaciated mountain ranges, dense forests, and exceptional variety of native plants and wildlife.

The Abel Tasman National Park is the smallest national park in New Zealand but probably the best known. It stretches along a stunning coastline of sandy, bush-edged beaches between rocky headlands. This unique coast track can take three to five days to walk or can be combined with a boat trip.

St Arnaud, on the shores of Lake Rotoiti, is a 90-minute drive from Nelson city through beautiful native forests. It is the gateway to the Nelson Lakes National Park, which includes Lake Rotoroa. This area is renowned for its brown trout fishing.

Nelson city is the biggest urban centre in the region, with Richmond only 14 kilometres away on the edge of the Waimea Plains. There are several museums in the area, the major one being Nelson Provincial Museum in Stoke. Many craftspeople and artists live in this region and more than 40 local art and craft galleries display and sell pottery, woodcraft, glass, paintings, jewellery and textiles.

Motueka, in the heart of the Nelson district, is the fruit belt of the region with apple and pear orchards, vineyards, berry fruit, hop gardens and stone fruit. The hills of Kahurangi National Park rise up behind Motueka.

Over the Takaka Hills and past Marble Mountain lies Golden Bay, about two hours' drive from Nelson. Takaka is the main town. The seaside settlement of Collingwood, further up the coast, is on the way to Farewell Spit, an amazing, 35-kilometre sandspit which is a bird sanctuary and wetland. Visit the clear freshwater springs of Waikoropupu (or Pupu Springs, as it is called locally), explore the Labyrinth Rocks and Te Anaroa Caves or feed the Anatoki eels, a pastime that has been popular for almost a hundred years.

The sweeping golden sands of Totaranui Beach in the Abel Tasman National Park.

Right: A sperm whale preparing to dive off Kaikoura.

Below: The crystal clear freshwater springs of Waikoropupu (or Pupu Springs) near Takaka.

Opposite: Lake Rotoiti, Nelson Lakes National Park.

The West Coast
and the Alpine Passes

The West Coast of the South Island stretches 600 kilometres along the rugged Tasman coastline and offers widely diverse landscapes. Here you can see fertile farmland, towns, deserted gold settlements, indigenous forests, dramatic coastlines, lowland river valleys, glaciers, roaring rivers, serene lakes, and the high, snow-capped peaks of the Southern Alps.

The area contains five national parks — Paparoa, Arthur's Pass, Mt Cook, Westland and Mt Aspiring National Parks, and a world heritage area in the south-west. The community spirit is strong amongst the 'Coasters', thanks to the West Coast's early isolation and consequent pioneer spirit.

Maori tribes are thought to have arrived in the region about eight hundred years ago in search of pounamu (greenstone or jade, for which the area is well known). Later, in the 1860s, Europeans arrived with hopes of finding gold; many settlements sprang up then, and some of these historic sites can be seen today.

The area is accessed by spectacularly scenic routes, whether by the Buller Gorge from Nelson, the Lewis Pass via Reefton, the new viaduct over Arthur's Pass from Christchurch, or the Haast Pass from Queenstown. A highlight of a visit to the West Coast is to traverse the spectacular, rugged and diverse landscapes of the Southern Alps on the *TransAlpine Express*.

Below: The rugged Paparoa National Park coastline.

Opposite: Pancake Rocks 'blowhole' at Punakaiki, Paparoa National Park.

From the north the West Coast begins at Karamea, at the edge of the Heaphy Track in Kahurangi National Park.

Down the coast at Westport the swift Buller River reaches the sea from its beginnings at Lake Rotoiti. This is the country's main source of bituminous coal. Cape Foulwind, just to the south of Westport, is known for its seal colony. Go inland to the small junction and farming settlement of Inangahua, 47 kilometes inland from Westport on the Buller River. At the height of the goldrush there were over a thousand miners at work in the tributaries of the Inangahua. The town of Reefton, where the roads from Greymouth and Westport converge on their way to Canterbury, owes its origins to the discovery of extensive gold-bearing quartz reefs in the 1800s. With this boom in mining came technology and innovation: in 1888, Reefton was the first town in the southern hemisphere to have electric lighting — in fact before New York or London! Surrounding Reefton is Victoria Conservation Park, the largest forest park in New Zealand, with rugged granite mountains and beech forests. There are plenty of miners' tracks, abandoned mines and historic sites to be explored.

In the Paparoa National Park is Punakaiki, noted for its pancake rocks and blowholes. These limestone stacks can put on a spectacular display, throwing up columns of spray with accompanying thundering sounds on an incoming tide with a westerly wind blowing. Visit the limestone caves, best done with a local guide, or take the lower Pororari River walk, which passes through subtropical forest and a limestone gorge.

Blackball, founded in 1864, was originally a base for transient goldhunters before becoming a settlement for coalminers. Greymouth is the major town on the West Coast and is situated at the mouth of the Grey River in a valley of limestone hills. The town takes its name from the river, which is itself named after Sir George Grey, twice governor and once prime minister of New Zealand. The town has an infamous cold wind known as 'the barber' because it feels like the cold edge of a barber's razor and is just as cutting.

Inland from Greytown is Lake Brunner, with the popular resort of Moana nestled just

Above: *Lake Brunner, West Coast.*
Opposite: *A grove of nikau palms, Paparoa National Park.*

below the Southern Alps on the lake's shores. From here there are wonderful bush walks and historic sites, as well as glow-worm grottos and wildlife at the Moana Zoo and Conservation Park.

Hokitika, at the mouth of the Hokitika River, was once the capital of the goldfields with most of the prospectors arriving through its bustling port to set up shanty settlements. Now these heady goldrush days are over, the local economy of Hokitika relies on forestry and the processing of minerals, in particular pounamu. Each year in February thousands of visitors flock to Hokitika for the Hokitika Wild Foods Festival which specialises in gourmet 'bush tucker'.

The northern gateway to the south-west New Zealand world heritage area, Te Wahi Pounamu, is Whataroa, near the kotuku (white heron) sanctuary. There are very few kotuku in New Zealand and they nest in a single colony near the outlet of the Whataroa River.

The townships of Fox and Franz Josef are about 25 kilometres apart and each about five kilometres from their respective glaciers. They nestle in the rainforest at the foot of steep mountains and give the visitor a base from which to participate in the many activities in the region. Both glaciers descend approximately 2,500 metres over 13 kilometres and are easily accessible. There are unguided and guided walks to the terminal face of both glaciers, to suit all ability levels. Lake Matheson, six kilometres west of Fox Glacier township, is renowned for perfectly reflecting images of Mt Cook and Mt Tasman in its mirror-smooth waters.

The drive south from the glaciers takes you into the heart of the world heritage area on the way to Haast. Enjoy panoramic views of the wild and rugged coastline at Knight Point. Just past Haast junction are historic Jackson's Bay and the Hapuka Estuary walk at Haast Beach. The road joining south Westland to Queenstown uses the Haast Pass, which is 563 metres above sea level.

Left: The Haast River at Haast Pass, with the southern rata in full summer bloom.

Below: Waimakariri River, Arthur's Pass National Park.

Opposite: Franz Josef Glacier, Westland National Park.

Lake Matheson, Westland National Park

Christchurch and Canterbury

Christchurch, the largest city in the South Island, is surrounded by the Cashmere Hills and the farmlands of Canterbury and is the aerial gateway to the rest of the South Island and Antarctica.

The city of Christchurch has the reputation for being 'more English than the English' with its many beautiful leafy parks, neo-Gothic cathedral, old stone buildings and tree-lined Avon River meandering through its centre.

Worth visiting in Christchurch are the International Antarctic Centre, the Christchurch Arts Centre, and Hagley Park. A ticket for the Christchurch tramway will provide you with a historic 25-minute tram ride around the city, stopping at some of the inner city's attractions.

Over the Port Hills is Lyttelton, the major port in the South Island, just 13 kilometres to the south of Christchurch through the Lyttleton–Christchurch tunnel, built in 1964. Lyttelton has a historic downtown area with the Anglican Church dating back to 1860. A prominent landmark is the Timeball Station with its Victorian mechanism that daily, for 58 years, signalled the time to

Below: A punter on the Avon River, Christchurch.

Opposite: A Christchurch tram in New Regent Street.

ships in the harbour by the dropping of a ball down the mast on the top of the tower. This allowed ships in the harbour to set their clocks and thereby accurately calculate longitude.

The road from Lyttelton runs to Governors Bay and on to Banks Peninsula. The village of Akaroa was founded by French whalers in 1838, and has a distinct French atmosphere.

To the north-west of Christchurch is Hanmer Springs, in the Hurunui region, well known for its outdoor thermal pools. This alpine village also offers the visitor skiing, mountain biking, walking tracks and jet boating. Further south is Mt Hutt, about 90 minutes from Christchurch, making it one of the closest ski-fields to this city with the country's longest ski season. The town of Methven is the nearest to Mt Hutt and the main service centre for the ski-fields, situated at the crossroads of six roads near the Rakaia River gorge. The Rakaia River, like the Waimakariri River, has an interesting formation in that it spreads over a wide area, fanning out in braids over a shingle bed, and is well known for its salmon fishing.

South-west of Christchurch, the area around Ashburton is well known for its magnificent fishing for salmon and sea-run trout in the Rakaia, Rangitata, and Ashburton Rivers. Another 70-odd kilometres further south is Timaru, where you can turn off to Lake Tekapo and Mt Cook National Park in the rugged tussock land, of the Mackenzie country. Lake Tekapo, like Lake Pukaki, Lake Ohau and other lakes in the region, has brilliant blue-green waters and is fed by glaciers (and is therefore too cold to swim in). It stretches for almost 20 kilometres north from the dam-controlled outlet at the village of Tekapo. The Church of the Good Shepherd, built by the lake in 1935, is a memorial to the pioneers of the Mackenzie country. It is built out of stones, shingle and sand from the shores of the lake.

From its east window the lake and mountain can be seen to best advantage in the early morning and later afternoon.

The grandeur of Mt Cook (Aorangi or Aoraki, 3,754 metres) beside Mt Tasman (3,117 metres) rises above the panoramic landscape of the Mt Cook National Park. Mt Cook is the highest peak in Australasia. Outdoor adventurers will be tempted by a myriad of activities in the park, including tramping, bushwalking, mountaineering and fishing during the summer months and glacier skiing in the winter. Scenic flights over the Alps are popular, with helicopters landing on the glaciers for sightseers or skiers. A famous and unique feature of the area's flora is the Mt Cook lily, which has a pure white flower. Many native birds are also found in this area including the kea (native parrot), New Zealand pigeon (kereru) and morepork (ruru), although the last of these, being nocturnal, is more often heard than seen.

Opposite above: Canterbury Cathedral, Cathedral Square.

Opposite below: The French settlement of Akaroa on Banks Peninsula.

Left: The majestic peak of Mt Cook/Aoraki (3,754m) overlooking Lake Pukaki.

Below: Highway 73 from Christchurch across the Southern Alps to the West Coast.

Central Otago

The Central Otago region covers a vast area of land bordering Otago to the east, Southland to the south, Fiordland and Mt Aspiring National Parks and the Southern Alps to the west and South Canterbury to the north.

Central Otago has a rich and very colourful past. In early times when explorers first set foot on the land the terrain was, in places, impassable, with high speargrass that had to be burnt to the ground to make progress. The landscapes of Central Otago offer dramatic contrasts throughout, with glacier-rounded hills, jagged peaks on mountain ranges, river torrents running through huge gorges and breathtaking, serene lakes.

The land wears the scars of its rugged and colourful past, and reminders of the goldrush days are evident in the old buildings that remain today. The Blue Lake at St Bathans was created as a result of sluicing for gold. The lake is used for recreational purposes today and the old Vulcan Hotel is still standing. In the pioneering days of last century, goldminers from all over the world descended upon the gold-rich rivers of Central Otago, spawning many small towns.

The village of Arrowtown, near Queenstown, has not only survived since that era (around 1862) but has become a thriving memorial to the area's rich history.

To the early settlers, the land and seasonal climates were extreme, with bitterly cold winters and scorching hot summers, but the settlers' pioneering spirit saw them through. Such was the case for William Rees (1827–1898); on his historic journey from Moeraki, on the east coast near Dunedin, to Queenstown the going got so tough that three

Below: Lake Wanaka at dusk.

Opposite: Vulcan Hotel at St Bathans, Central Otago.

Autumn colours near Arrowtown.

A lake frozen solid near Lake Hayes, Central Otago.

of his party of five had to turn back, leaving only Rees and one other to continue.

The colours of Central Otago's landscape can vary dramatically depending on the time of year but during autumn they are spectacular.

There are many lakes and rivers in the region. The Clutha River, which flows out of Lake Wanaka, eventually weaving its way down country through several hydroelectric dams to reach the sea at Balclutha, on the south-eastern coastline just south of Dunedin, is New Zealand's largest river by volume and is 338 kilometres long. The rivers in Central Otago always provide plenty of opportunity for trout or salmon fishing, but anglers need to ensure they obtain a fishing licence first from a fishing tackle shop.

The economy of the region is built on large sheep stations in the high country, pipfruit orchards on lower ground, and tourism. Tourism plays the biggest role in the economy as Central Otago's stunning landscape continues to attract visitors from the world over. Queenstown is 'the jewel in the crown' and one of New Zealand's most popular inland holiday destinations.

When touring through Central Otago during summer months, you will always find a plentiful supply of pipfruit on sale from the many orchards at the roadside.

Opposite: The snow-clad
tussock landscape
at Lindis Pass.

Left: Lake Wakatipu and
The Remarkables at dusk.

Below: Lake Hawea
during summer.

*Looking west from Queenstown up
Lake Wakatipu towards
Walter Peak at sunset.*

Queenstown

Queenstown is located on the foreshore of Lake Wakatipu in the Southern Lakes region of Central Otago. It is completely surrounded by majestic mountain ranges, so the scenery changes dramatically with the seasons.

Below: Queenstown Bay with the snow-covered Remarkables in the background.

Opposite: The sheer exhilaration of jet boating down the Kawarau River with The Remarkables in the background.

Seen steaming on Lake Wakatipu is the TSS *Earnslaw*, affectionately known as 'the Lady of the Lake'. Built in 1912, it holds a special place in the hearts of the Queenstown people. She plied the lake providing a regular service carrying stock and supplies to runholders until 1969, when the Railways Department sold her to a private company which now uses it to carry visitors for cruises on the lake. One of the *Earnlaw*'s great trips today is the cruise across Lake Wakatipu to Walter Peak High Country Farm Station for either a daytime or evening excursion.

Standing 446 metres high above Queenstown is Bob's Peak. A gondola rises from Queenstown virtually vertically up the rocky, partially tree-covered cliff-face to the terminal where there is a breathtaking panorama of Lake Wakatipu and the surrounding alpine landscape.

There are many exciting adventure activities to be had in the Queenstown and Southern Lakes region. Those seeking an adrenalin rush may wish to try the Skyline Luge, a fast ride down a steep winding incline on a luge cart, or a bungy jump.

TSS Earnslaw '*Lady of the Lake*' cruises
round Queenstown Bay.

Fiordland

Fiordland, in the south-west corner of New Zealand, makes up most of the Te Wahipounamu World Heritage Area, and Fiordland National Park within it is one of the largest national parks in the country at 1,257,000 hectares. The park's rugged coastline comprises 16 sounds weaving their way inland.

Here you will find a true wilderness with rugged snow-capped mountains, glacial lakes and valleys, fiords, magnificent waterfalls, dense rainforest and alpine tussock. Bottlenose dolphins, fur seals and crested penguins abound in the sounds and kea, tui, bellbirds and wood pigeons fly free in the forests. The Fiordland crested penguin, with a bright yellow plume on its head, is unique to New Zealand and commonly sighted in colonies on the western seaboard in the Fiordland and Westland National Parks. In Maori legend, the fiords were not created by rivers of ice, but by Tu Te Raki Whanoa, a god-like figure who came here wielding a magical adze and uttering incantations. Milford Sound (Piopiotahi) is without doubt his finest creation.

Fiordland National Park is accessed through Te Anau, on the shores of Lake Te Anau, and called New Zealand's 'walking capital' because of its proximity to the Hollyford, Routeburn and Milford tracks. Luxury coaches, with specially designed glass roofs for viewing the majestic mountains, depart Queenstown daily for a pleasant day trip to Milford Sound which can include a scenic cruise on the sound. There are also aircraft services departing from Queenstown and Wanaka to Milford Sound. The terrain in Fiordland is extremely rugged and virtually inaccessible. Its lush green plant life luxuriates in the heavy rainfall here — about 7270 millimetres a year, making this region one

Below: Mirror Lakes, Fiordland National Park.

Opposite: A rainstorm adds to the torrents flowing over Stirling Falls, falling the height of a fourteen-story building into the deep waters of Milford Sound.

Above: The picture-perfect mirror image of Mitre Peak at Milford Sound.
Opposite: Mt Talbot, Fiordland National Park.

of the wettest in the world. However, the thought of the heavy rainfall should not deter visitors to the area: with its cascading waterfalls falling from thousands of metres, the landscape is as dramatic in heavy rains as it is on still calm days when mirror images of towering mountain peaks are reflected in the tranquil waters of the fiords.

The fiords were formed thousands of years ago when the sea entered deeply excavated glacial troughs or valleys after the ice had melted away, leaving sea walls that rise 1200 metres vertically from the sea.

Below the water the fiord walls continue their sheer vertical drop to depths of over 250 metres, where black coral can be found. Milford Sound, part of the Te Wahipounamu World Heritage Area, is also a marine reserve and is considered by marine biologists to be one of the most diverse and interesting marine ecosystems in the world. From just 15 metres below the water surface Milford Sound's rock walls become covered with large numbers of spectacular black colonies up to three metres in height which are over 200 years old. They comprise the largest black coral population in the world. There are many other varieties of colourful marine life carpeting the walls of the fiord, including red or precious corals, sea fans, feather stars, sponges, spiny lobsters, octopuses, sea squirts and more. Large numbers of colourful fish congregate along the walls, including trumpeter, groper, leatherjackets and large schools of telescope fish. There are over 180 different species of fish present in the fiord. This wonderful underwater seascape can be viewed in a deep-diving submersible to depths of 180 metres. This submarine operates during daylight hours all year round in Milford Sound.

Milford Sound at sunset.

Dunedin

Dunedin is an historic university city on the east coast of the South Island. Its population increases by 20 per cent during term time. The city spreads around the shores of the sheltered harbour that the city's Scottish ancestors first sailed up some 160 years ago. To the east of the city are white sandy beaches with wild surf, huge cliffs and sheltered harbours; to the south, lush farmland; and to the west, the tussock-covered hills of Central Otago.

Below: Dunedin Railway Station.

Right: The stormy ocean pounds the rocky coastline below the Taiaroa Lighthouse at the heads to Otago Harbour.

Dunedin is the Celtic word for Edinburgh, and its Scottish heritage makes it the 'Edinburgh of the South': it has the only kilt shop in the country and produces the only New Zealand whisky.

The cityscape of Dunedin includes Victorian and Edwardian spires of neo-Gothic buildings made from grey stone. The University of Otago was New Zealand's first university, built in 1878 from blue stone with a slate roof. Its clock tower is now preserved by the Historic Places Trust.

A tour of the city could begin at the Octagon, the eight-sided garden chosen for the city centre in 1846 with its statue of Robbie Burns and Dunedin Public Art Gallery. Fine examples of Victorian and Edwardian architecture can be found in the city centre, including the Dunedin Railway Station, Olveston House, the University of Otago and the Otago Settlers' Museum with its Southern Land, Southern People gallery. The world's steepest road is at Baldwin Street, and from Signal Hill there are spectacular

Right: Dunedin's Municipal Chambers with St Pauls Cathedral to the left, forming part of the Octagon in the city centre.

Below: Larnach Castle on Otago Peninsula.

Opposite above: New Zealand's rarest penguin, the yellow-eyed penguin (hoiho), lives on the eastern and southern coasts of the South Island.

Opposite below: Tunnel Beach, Otago coastline, Dunedin.

views of the city, the harbour and Otago Peninsula.

A drive out to the Otago Peninsula is worthwhile, along stonewalled Highcliff Road beside the Pacific Ocean with its harbour and beautiful beaches. Larnach Castle, built in 1871 by William Larnach, is situated in 30 acres of wonderfully landscaped gardens and farmland. This castle, positioned high above the harbour, is a Victorian masterpiece with a lookout turret offering 360-degree views of the city, ocean and surrounding countryside. It is worth visiting Glenfalloch Woodland Gardens (also on the peninsula), especially during mid-September to October when many flowering plants are at their best. Further on towards Taiaroa Head is the Portobello Marine Laboratory and Aquarium. The aquarium displays an amazing array of sea life including sea horses, colourful sponges, sea squirts, anemones, sea slugs, octopuses and common fish species.

On the end of the peninsula is Taiaroa Head, home of the royal albatross colony. Directly behind the centre is Taiaroa Head Lighthouse standing high above the jagged cliff-face and the stormy sea below.

For a great view of Otago Harbour and its wildlife, take a trip on the Monarch Wildlife Cruise to see albatrosses, penguins, seals, shags and other ocean birds in their natural enviroment.

The Catlins

The Catlins district is situated on the south-east coast of New Zealand, well off the beaten track, on the southern scenic route. The area was named after a whaling ship's captain who bought a large amount of land on the coast and inland from local Maori.

The Maori were attracted to the region because of its abundance of food — the sea and rivers for fish and the forests for hunting, especially the moa (a large flightless bird, now extinct). Most of the early settlements were centred around whaling stations during the 1830s but saw-milling gradually became the sustaining industry during those early years. The farming town of Owaka is now the centre of the Catlins district. A good day trip from Owaka is the river walk in the Catlins Forest Park.

Cathedral Caves can be visited only between the hour before and the hour after low tide. They rise more than 30 metres in places and are a series of interlocking sea caves. At Curio Bay there is an ancient geological phenomenon of great significance, the petrified forest where fossilised trees such as kauri and matai lie embedded in rock. These are the remains of a Jurassic-age forest from 180 million years ago. Slope Point is the southernmost point of the South Island of New Zealand with windswept rugged beaches.

There are many waterfalls in this region. Worth noting are Purakaunui Falls, which cascade 20 metres over three terraces, McLean Falls, Matai Falls and Niagara Falls.

Nugget Point is notable for its lighthouse, built in 1869, and as a breeding ground for fur seals, sea lions, gannets, shooty shearwaters, shags, and the yellow-eyed penguin. The Catlins has an abundance of native birds, with many sea, estuary and forest birds, including rare and endangered species.

Below: Purakaunui Falls, Catlins.

Opposite: Cathedral Caves, coastal Catlins.

Eruption at Mt Ruapehu
Page i: *Mitre Peak, Milford Sound.*
Page ii: *Marokopa Falls, King Country*

ISBN 1-86958-887-8

© 2001 Original text and photographs — David Kerr
The moral rights of the author have been asserted

© 2001 Design and format — Hodder Moa Beckett Publishers Ltd

First published in 2001 by Hodder Moa Beckett Publishers Ltd
[a member of the Hodder Headline Group],
4 Whetu Place, Mairangi Bay, Auckland, New Zealand

Reprinted 2004

Designed and produced by Hodder Moa Beckett Publishers Ltd
Film and colour separations by Microdot, Auckland
Printed by Everbest Printing Co., Ltd, China